Team *Emotional &* *Social* Intelligence

Participant
Workbook

TESI® Short

Marcia Hughes &
James Bradford Terrell

Pfeiffer®
An Imprint of
WILEY

Published by Pfeiffer
An Imprint of Wiley
989 Market Street, San Francisco, CA 94103-1741
www.pfeiffer.com

For additional copies/bulk purchases of this book in the U.S. please contact 800-274-4434.

Pfeiffer books and products are available through most bookstores. To contact Pfeiffer directly call our Customer Care Department within the U.S. at 800-274-4434, outside the U.S. at 317-572-3985, fax 317-572-4002, or visit www.pfeiffer.com.

Pfeiffer also publishes its books in a variety of electronic formats. Some content that appears in print may not be available in electronic books.

ISBN 978-0-7879-8845-6

Acquiring Editor: Holly Allen   Editor: Rebecca Taff
Director of Development: Kathleen Dolan Davies   Editorial Assistant: Marisa Kelley
Developmental Editor: Susan Rachmeler   Manufacturing Supervisor: Becky Morgan
Production Editor: Dawn Kilgore

Printed in the United States of America
Printing   10 9 8 7 6 5 4 3 2 1

CONTENTS

TEAMS ARE THE ENGINES that run our business, our community, perhaps ultimately our world. Work and play are organized around teams to gain powerful performance results and to satisfy our needs to interact as social beings. Teams shine when they are capable of expanding their understanding, connection, commitment, and courage. Lucky members of these teams enjoy their experience of working together; thus, their creative juices flow and the organization benefits from their enhanced productivity. Another benefit when teams function in synch is improved employee retention.

We are privileged to have the opportunity to work with you, a team member. We honor your work and your learning process. It is our hope that the seven skills of emotional and social intelligence will help you recognize strengths and new possibilities. Have fun as you work with your team—life is better that way, and it's a great way to learn.

During this workshop, you will have the opportunity to answer questions about how you see your team functioning in the seven core skills of emotional and social intelligence by taking the TESI® Short. You will be guided to take time to reflect on your observations, to learn from one another, and to learn how to improve your team skills.

We would be honored to continue the learning journey with you. Visit our websites, www.cgrowth.com and www.TheEmotionallyIntelligentTeam.com, to join our ezine list, gain more information on developing your Team ESI, and learn about the TESI® in a longer version.

Good luck in your journey!
Marcia Hughes and James Terrell

Welcome, Introductions, and Objectives

In order to have a winner, the team must have a feeling of unity; every player must put the team first—ahead of personal glory.

Paul Bear Bryant

My Desired Outcome

Think about what you want to get out of this workshop for yourself and your team.

All the forces in the world are not as powerful as an idea
whose time has come.

                                          Victor Hugo

This workshop focuses on the seven skills central to developing your team's behaviors of success. These are the key skills your team and teams like yours need to be effective to meet the growing challenges you face.

Workshop Objectives

Our purpose today is to gauge and begin expanding your emotional and social effectiveness as a team. Our objectives in building this team success are two-fold:

- To recognize your team's current emotional and social effectiveness
- To commit to becoming more effective in one or two of the seven skills by developing an action plan

Understanding and enhancing your team's Emotional and Social Intelligence (ESI) is a force whose time has come. Yet the process will only support your team in relation to the attention and commitment you make individually and as a team.

Clarifying your sense of the value of the workshop for you and for your team is a great way for you to determine how to gain the most from the process for both you and your team. In the space provided below, record your thoughts about your own objectives for today as well as the objectives of your team.

Notes on My Objectives for This Workshop

Notes on the Team's Objectives for This Workshop

2

What Is a Team? What Is ESI? Bringing Them Together

How would you define a team?

Definition of a Team

A team is a group of two or more people who interdependently seek to meet a common purpose, often through solving problems, in order to meet their own and their organization's goals. At a minimum, a team should be a cooperative unit and, at its best, a team is a collaborative unit.

Given this definition, do you feel you are a team?

Are there times when you act more like a group of individuals working alone than like a team?

Do you have any other components you would add to the definition of a team?

Team emotional and social intelligence (ESI) is defined as the ability to recognize and manage your own emotions and to recognize and respond effectively to those of others. The concept includes understanding your engagement with others from the "big picture" point of view and the ability to direct change and to adapt to that change.

3

Take the TESI® Short Survey

Follow the facilitator's directions and the directions in the TESI® Short Survey to take and score the survey.

After the personal and group scoring are complete, respond to the following questions.

Overall Assessment: How I See My Team

What are the areas of team strength? What makes these areas our strengths?

What are my team's challenges? What could we improve? Why would it serve us and our organization to improve?

What areas have the largest range of scoring. Why was that?

Do my teammates see the team functioning the same as I do? Record your thoughts about differences and similarities below.

4

Discuss Results

Two purposes in reviewing results:

- To understand the team's current functioning
- To note what you (or the team) can improve

How effectively is the team functioning overall?

List two reasons why you just answered the way you did.

What is your first impression of the skill you believe would be best for the team to improve?

5

The Collaborative Growth® Team Model

Understanding and developing the behaviors of success requires that team members develop and utilize the seven core ESI skills shown in the outer circle of this figure. This will lead to the four results shown in the middle circle and the universally sought after benefits of sustainable productivity and emotional and social well-being for the team and its members.

From Emotional Intelligence to Collaborative Intelligence™
A Team Model

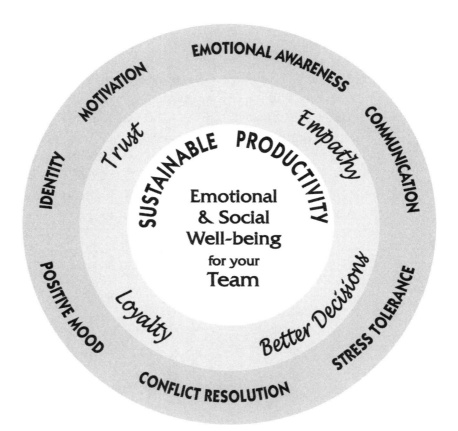

Definitions

Team

A team is a group of two or more people who interdependently seek to meet a common purpose, often through solving problems, in order to meet their own and their organization's goals. At a minimum, a team should be a cooperative unit and, at its best, a team is a collaborative unit.

Emotional and Social Intelligence (ESI)

Emotional and social intelligence reflects the ability to recognize and manage your own emotions and to recognize and respond effectively to those of others. It includes understanding your engagement with others from the "big picture" point of view and the ability to direct change and to adapt to that change.

Collaborative Intelligence™

Collaboration is a composite skill that emerges from the masterful use of your ESI skills. The members of a football team collaborate when they huddle and agree that they will each do his part to execute a particular play. In the middle of the play, except in the face of an unexpected opportunity, the fullback won't decide to change the play because he'd prefer to run the ball rather than block! Team loyalty is unquestioned. When your team collaborates, you take time to explore alternative answers and find a solution that integrates the wisdom of the team. It takes more time up-front, because you invest in listening to one another, to thinking things through, and to coordinating the execution of your response with genuine respect for one another. Collaboration pays off big time as you and your team progress. Your self-discipline and collective intuition as a team will make the future much easier to navigate because teams that coordinate their ESI skills naturally act with Collaborative Intelligence™.

This set of coordinated competencies is the birthplace of synergy. Teams tap into their shared memories and individual capacities to maximize their knowledge, problem-solving capabilities, and resilience. They respond with agility to the fluctuating emotional and social contexts of the team and the organizational dynamics. The correct blend of ESI skills is the rocket fuel that propels your team to achieve its full collaborative capacity.

What does Collaborative Intelligence™ mean to you?

What skills do you feel that your team is using well enough to be considered a high-level collaborative experience?

What are the differences in outcomes you find when you collaborate?

Notes on the Team Model and Definitions

6

The Seven Skills of Your Team's ESI

Each of the seven ESI skills plays a big part in your team's effectiveness and how much you enjoy working within your team. The skills are presented in a circle because each skill interacts with all the others. No real relationship in a team happens in isolation.

Team Identity

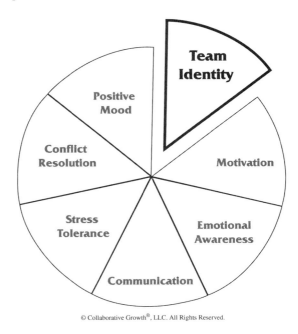

Two Key Aspects of Team Identity

The first goal when a team forms is for each team member to find something about the team that is similar to something about him- or herself. For example, you might say, "The team is upbeat and I'm upbeat." When team members have identified with the team, the team becomes a problem-solving organism that is larger than the sum of its parts. The second aspect of team identity is the view of the team as a whole, both as seen by others and as seen by the team itself. When your team has a clarified sense of purpose, it should be fairly easy to understand why you are on that team and to identify with your teammates. Without the sense of purpose, you may just be attending meetings.

What are some of the views held about your team? Which ones are internal, coming from within? Which ones come from others?

Ingredients Making Up Team Identity

1. Sense of purpose

2. Acceptance of one another

3. Perception that the team is a distinct entity

4. Commitment to the team and its purpose

5. Pride in the team

6. Clarity of roles and responsibilities

7. Resilience, including the recognition of the reality that things change

Notes on Shared Stories

What is your identity with the team? What do you tell others about being on this team?

Is your connection strong, weak, or in between? Why?

Do you want to change your connection?

How strong is the team's identity as an average score?

Exercise: Focusing on Our Team's Purpose

In your subgroups, write your responses to the following on flip-chart paper:

- The team's purpose

- Who or what the team affects the most and where the team has the greatest impact

- What each person feels is best about what the team does

You'll have five minutes for this task. When you have finished, be prepared to share your responses with the rest of the group and to discuss actionable items.

Key Learnings on Team Identity

Motivation

Team motivation is exemplified by your team's commitment to activate its three essential resources of time, energy, and intelligence—both IQ and ESI. Teams tap into motivation via the internal state of each member; the mixture of these states form the drive for the team to execute its plan of action.

Your TESI® Short results give feedback on the energy levels within your team, sense of responsibility within the team, and whether competition is working for, or against, the team.

What do your think your TESI® Short results indicate about your team energy level?

Ingredients Making Up Motivation

The seven ingredients that form the recipe for motivating your team are first based in the people—the members of the team. Recognizing each member and the skills he or she brings creates the opportunity to bring the gifts each one has to contribute to life. A team that recognizes the needs and desires of team members builds the capacity and desire to act. It's like pulling the curtains to find many doorways ready to open to potential contributions to support the team. A team needs goals as a means of organizing, mutually agreed-on targets, and a sense of being on the same page. If your team is operating from many different directions, you're more likely to step on one another's toes than to make progress. Keep one another accountable, reinforce success, and be doggedly persistent in your movement toward any goal that's truly important for the team. If it isn't important, consider getting rid of it.

> **The Seven Ingredients of Motivation**
> 1. People
> 2. Needs
> 3. Desires
> 4. Goals
> 5. Accountability
> 6. Reinforcement
> 7. Persistence

Notes on Shared Stories

On a scale of 1 to 10, 10 being highest, how much motivation do you contribute to the team?

Is there a stretch goal your team could take on that would be exciting to undertake? If not, what current goal(s) energize you or the team?

How do you help one another do your best? What more could you do?

Exercise: Our Favorite Goal

The facilitator will let you know whether you'll discuss the following questions as a whole group or in a subgroup. If using subgroups, be prepared to share the key points of your discussion with the whole group later on.

List the team's goals.

Which one or two of these goals are most motivating? Why?

What have you learned about what motivates you? How can you apply that back on the job?

Key Learnings on Motivation

Emotional Awareness

The exercise of team emotional awareness requires members of the team to notice one another's emotions, to seek to understand why each emotion exists when it is relevant to the team engagement, and to respond appropriately.

Your TESI® Short results measure the amount of attention your team pays to noticing, understanding, and respecting feelings of team members. This is a critical factor in motivation, productivity, and your ability to collaborate. With emotional awareness, you gain considerable data that supports the success of your team. Without that information, you are leaving lots of valuable data on the table.

Ingredients Making Up Emotional Awareness

As team members sharpen their skills in emotional awareness, six ingredients will influence your success. Given that emotions are an unavoidable part of human interaction, you will be more successful if you work with the information. Every team member will profit by developing comfort with emotions, increasing his or her capability in discerning others' emotions, and responding with compassion to one another. Start noticing the rich gradations of emotional response. When your teammate didn't like some activity recently, was he or she mildly annoyed, perturbed, frustrated, angry, or seething? There is considerable difference along this continuum. Take the high road in responding to one another. You increase the chance of building positive relationships and certainly diminish the possibility of discord.

The Six Ingredients of Emotional Awareness

1. Exploring and using the emotional information you receive from one another

2. Being comfortable with emotions

3. Being aware of a rich assortment of emotional behaviors

4. Discerning the gradations of various emotional responses

5. Being open to others' expression of emotion so you can understand them

6. Gracefully responding, even to emotions of team members that you don't understand or appreciate

Notes on Shared Stories

How do you work as a team? Does everyone have a reasonable opportunity to participate?

Do you value the differences team members bring to the table? Do you reflect understanding of one another if a team member has something major going on outside of the team?

Do you feel that team members understand you and the messages you seek to communicate about what is important to you? If not, what can you do to communicate better?

Have you experienced emotions to be contagious? What other emotions have you noticed to be contagious around your team?

Exercise: Identifying Emotions

When the facilitator tells you to, you'll have one minute to list as many emotions as you can think of.

List of emotions:

After you have had a chance to review the lists as a group, you'll break into subgroups and compose a story using five of the emotions. You'll have five minutes to create your story, which you should be prepared to share with the entire group. You can take notes below if you need to:

As a group, you'll discuss the following questions:

How do you notice and respond to others' emotions?

What are some ways that you can acknowledge others' emotions?

Key Learning on Emotional Awareness

Communication

Team communication is the process of sharing information to meet some need or desire in which one group or person sends a message that is received by another group or person and for which that sharing process has an impact for the team. Communication is what people do to connect with others so that they can satisfy their needs and desires to make life better.

Team communication is defined in the TESI® Short as providing feedback on how well team members listen, encourage participation, and discuss sensitive matters. It is of central importance for every kind of team interaction.

Ingredients Making Up Team Communication

To communicate, one person—the sender—must transmit information to someone else—the receiver. This message can go to the whole team or to one person, but there has to be an exchange of a message or there is no communication. Can you remember times when you thought you had described something well, but others say they've never heard of the topic? Of course, that's frustrating. It reflects the basic fact that communication did not occur. You've probably heard that communication is composed of both verbal and non-verbal components. The verbal part can be challenging, but it's easier than being really clear about the non-verbal messages you send. Be careful, your non-verbals are likely to tell the truth! If you want to seem trustworthy, you must be congruent with the messages you are sending.

All communication has meaning, be it trivial—"Please post a notice of our meeting"—or of huge consequence—"The building is on fire!" However, notice that those messages also have a feeling component that adds depth to the meaning. The difference in feeling behind these two sentences is great.

The final component in the list of ingredients of communication is technique. Just how do you communicate? You have a strategy, whether you're aware of it or not. It will behoove you to become aware of the techniques you're employing.

The Six Ingredients of Communication

1. Sender

2. Receiver

3. Message

4. Meaning

5. Feeling

6. Technique

Do you take time to listen to one another?

Do you take responsibility if your message isn't understood? It can be easy to blame others, but it doesn't really help, does it?

Do you let others know that you did listen to them? Do you provide reflective feedback and follow up with questions if you don't understand?

Exercise: Listening and Receiving

Think of something going on in your life that you care about at a moderate level—don't let it get too dramatic, but the story needs some emotional content.

In pairs, you'll take turns telling your stories. When you're the listener, be sure to listen, engage with the speaker, and offer reflective feedback—but don't take over.

After five minutes, switch roles.

After five minutes, discuss with your partner how the storytelling went.

As a group, you'll discuss the following questions:

- How did this activity feel? What worked? What didn't?
- Do you do this enough at the team level?
- Can you build more active listening into your team engagement? How?

Key Learnings on Communication

Stress Tolerance

Stress tolerance is one skill every team agrees is relevant for the team. In today's world, where demands on the workforce seem to constantly grow, developing skills to manage these expectations so they don't take a toll on your health or happiness is essential. What some team members don't realize is how much they can help one another in managing stress. Your team can do this through stress-releasing activities for the whole team—such as group stretching or brief relaxation sessions—and by being good role models for one another—by taking the stairs instead of the elevator, for example.

Stress tolerance skills give the team a reflection of how well it's doing in managing the pressures of workload, time constraints, and the real needs for work-life balance. This scale is the closest of all scales to physical health.

Ingredients Making Up Team Stress Tolerance

The seven ingredients that compose stress tolerance begin with being aware of your environment—that's your whole environment, the physical components as well as the emotional ones. Are people tense or at ease? Are you comfortable in your setting? If not, can you change it? This question demonstrates the importance of assertiveness (to protect yourself from the impact of stress) and self-regard (to know that you deserve it). When you individually and as a team develop your stress tolerance, your experience of wellness will include an expanding sense of work-life balance. Your sense of humor will improve and begin to lighten up the atmosphere at work and at home. Just how important is that project? Will it make a world-wide difference? Will it matter in several weeks or several years? Flexibility supports stress tolerance because it helps you be sufficiently resilient to find a variety of answers. Adding a dose of humility can help you slow down and be more compassionate with teammates. Being able to find a workaround when it seems like the team is stuck can make the difference between completing the project and leaving it undone.

The Seven Stress Tolerance Ingredients
1. Environmental awareness
2. Assertiveness
3. Self-regard
4. Wellness
5. Humor
6. Flexibility
7. Humility

Who on the team best models stress tolerance? What can he or she teach everyone?

Can you take turns helping one another gain perspective on just how important a project is?

How do you exercise flexibility as a team?

Exercise: Exploring Work-Life Balance

As a whole group, discuss the question, "What does work-life balance mean to you?"

Form pairs and tell each other about a hobby, activity, or interest you have. Be sure both of you participate. You have five minutes total.

As a whole group, discuss the question, "How can you support one another in taking time to keep diversity in your life as you develop your other interests?"

Key Learnings on Stress Tolerance

Conflict Resolution

Team conflict occurs when there is disagreement based on different perspectives, values, or priorities that rises to the level of disturbing the system to some degree. Conflict resolution is the process followed by the individuals and teams who are facing such a challenge. Many styles of resolution can be followed, including cooperation, confrontation, competition, and the most sophisticated—collaboration.

The TESI® Short addresses how constructively a team deals with disagreement and whether the team is able to deal with adversity to enhance its functioning, rather than being caught up in the conflict. Managing conflict and taking advantage of the awareness it can bring is essential for productivity.

We learn and grow through conflict. Any change will include some aspect of conflict as we face the change; however, when there is an easy shift or transition to a new way, we seldom think of it as conflict. When there's disagreement, a dispute, or disgruntlement, then we know there is conflict. The way team members respond to conflict has a significant impact on how effective a team is. If some members of the team, especially the team leader, are conflict-adverse, shying away from dealing with issues will undermine the team. Pretending an issue isn't there will never make it go away, but it can encourage passive/aggressive behavior that interferes with a team accomplishing its mission. No matter how much you or your team doesn't like conflict, you can learn how to work with it and how to answer the questions that need to be addressed. If this is a challenge area for your team, you will gain a great deal by enhancing your conflict-resolution skills.

Ingredients Making Up Conflict Resolution

The ingredients for resolving conflict begin with patience and the willingness to engage and to listen. Resolving conflict calls for having an intention to solve key issues and then pay attention to what is critical to achieving a solution. Teams that are able to solve problems recognize that each member brings a different perspective to the matter and use collaborative communication strategies to solve them. Such communication strategies require an artful combination of being assertive while showing empathy for one another. Teams benefit by understanding that there are many ways to deal with conflict so they can make good choices about how to address difficult matters, from the mundane to the critical. A sense of humor helps team members not take themselves or any problem too seriously. It helps open team members' thinking and their ability to recognize the possibilities of different solutions.

The Nine Ingredients of Conflict Resolution
1. Patience/willingness
2. Perspective
3. Intention/attention
4. Collaborative communication
5. Empathy
6. Assertiveness
7. Choice in conflict resolution style
8. Humor
9. Gratitude

Do you take advantage of different styles for resolving conflict, such as accommodation and collaboration? If yes, how? If not, why not?

Do you take time to step back and discuss how you solved a problem, to evaluate what worked and where you could benefit from making changes in your approach? Describe some of your results.

For those of you who would prefer to avoid conflict, who would you pair with on the team to improve your conflict engagement skills and why?

Exercise: Learning from Experience

Think of a problem you previously worked on in your team.

What process did you use to solve the problem?

Was this a good solution process that you would like to repeat? If so, how could you use this process more often? If not, what would you like to change in the process?

Key Learnings on Conflict Resolution

Positive Mood

Happiness and optimism are both aspects of having a positive mood and are vital parts of emotional and social intelligence. Happiness is based on your ability to be satisfied with what happens today. It reflects your ability to accept all that is here right now, embrace it, and be deeply grateful. Optimism is the team and team members' hopefulness about future outcomes. It is embodied in part by a team's can-do attitude.

The TESI® Short results on Positive Mood is a comment on the level of encouragement present, members' sense of humor, and how successful the team expects to be. These attributes are major support for a team's flexibility and resilience.

Ingredients Making Up Team Positive Mood

There are seven ingredients to building a team's positive mood. A predominant one is a positive attitude, often referred to as a "can-do" attitude. This is a strong indicator of optimism, as it helps team members believe that they can find successful and effective answers to challenges. A team with a strong positive mood will be hopeful about the future and grateful for what is going well today. The members will reflect a sense of curiosity about what else is possible. When big challenges arise, they will take the long-term view that builds perspective. Teams that have strength in positive mood have a sense of abundance—that good things happen to them. They will encourage playfulness in one another, and all of these skills build a sense of zest for the projects on the table and the possibilities in the future.

The Seven Ingredients of Positive Mood

1. Positive/can-do attitude

2. Hopefulness

3. Curiosity

4. Long-term view (perseverance)

5. Attitude of abundance

6. Playfulness

7. Zest

How do you demonstrate a can-do attitude as a team?

Do you have a good ability to take the long-term view and keep things in perspective? How do you demonstrate this?

Are playfulness and a sense of zest encouraged in your team? How?

Exercise: Building a Sense of Possibility

You'll have ten minutes for the paired portion of this exercise.

In pairs, list on a flip chart ten ways to use any of the seven ingredients to build the team's positive mood.

For each idea, rate the possibility of success as follows:

10 points   very likely to be successful

6 points   might be successful

1 point   not likely to be successful

Total your points.

As a group, discuss the ideas and ratings. Select two or three actions that the team wants to implement.

Key Learnings on Positive Mood

7

The Four Results for Your Team

From Emotional Intelligence to Collaborative Intelligence™
A Team Model

The four results you gain as you begin to strengthen the team's use of these seven skills are:

- Empathy
- Trust
- Loyalty
- Better Decisions

Empathy

What do you think empathy means?

Examples of empathy:

Why is empathy important for team success?

Team members are using their skill in empathy when they demonstrate care, concern, and respect to one another and others with whom they interact. Empathy includes demonstrating to someone that you took time to listen. This often happens by affirming key points of emphasis or by responding to a request. Empathy is multi-dimensional; it shows up as a component of some of the seven skills, such as communication and conflict resolution, and it deeply influences whether the other benefits develop in a team.

Trust

What do you think trust means?

Examples of trust:

Why is trust important for team success?

As stated in *The Emotionally Intelligent Team,* trust is the glue that holds teams together. Every component of a team's emotional or social intelligence (or lack thereof) is demonstrated by the depth and resilience of trust a team enjoys. Members of a team develop trust in one another when they receive continuous honest communication, when they feel that what is communicated is in their best interests, and when they feel safe. Trust occurs when team members are confident they can rely on one another. This energy creates strong bonds that support desired behaviors of risk taking and innovation.

Loyalty

What do you think loyalty means?

Examples of loyalty:

Why is loyalty important for team success?

Team members demonstrate loyalty to the team, and the team demonstrates loyalty to the organization, when they have sufficient data to understand expectations and know they will be treated respectfully and be acknowledged. When these circumstances come to bear, they develop allegiance to the team or organization. Key behaviors that must be demonstrated by the organization, the leaders, and other team members to gain this beneficial result include constancy, reliability, fidelity, honesty, and acknowledgment of the value of each member of the team as well as the team as a whole.

Better Decisions

What do you think better decisions are?

Examples of better decisions:

Why are better decisions important for team success?

Your team exists in order to solve problems, to make decisions, and to get things done. When a team applies the seven ESI skills, the decisions are more long-lasting. This is true because the members communicate, have fun, and engage in creative conflict sufficiently to test possible solutions and find the best answers. In fact, better decisions are a natural consequence of the collaborative process.

8

The Two Lasting Benefits of Sustainable Success for Your Team

From Emotional Intelligence to Collaborative Intelligence™
A Team Model

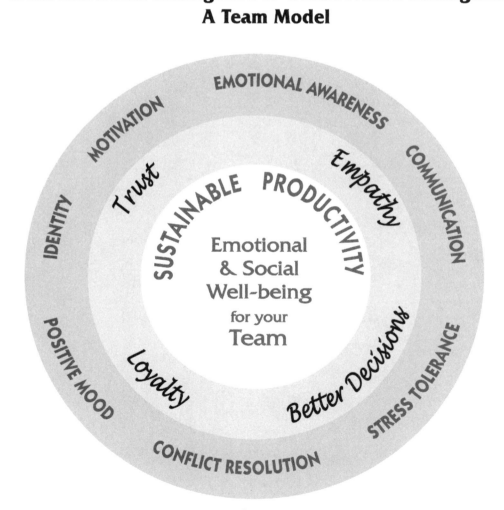

As the seven team skills are strengthened and the four results develop, your team will begin experiencing what every team and organization supporting the team wants— sustainable productivity and emotional and social well-being within the team.

Sustainable Productivity

A well-oiled machine designed for the right job will produce long-term superior output. So will a team that's "firing on all cylinders," because the members are exercising their ESI muscles, treating one another respectfully, and focusing on creative ways of accomplishing their jobs.

Emotional and Social Well-Being

"Emotional and social well-being manifests when team members have each found the perfect pitch in their interactions and resonates in a powerful and harmonious chord. This awesome feeling becomes a sustainable part of team life when everyone shares the intention to apply the seven ESI skills and treats each day as a new opportunity built on a history of increased openness and commitment to results. This kind of optimism is the sustainable fuel of great teamwork."

From *The Emotionally Intelligent Team*, Hughes and Terrell, 2007

Notes

9

Action Planning

Write down the one or two skills for which you'll be creating an action plan:

As a group, discuss the steps team members or the team as a whole can take to develop each of the skills. (You may wish to review your notes, particularly the key learnings section for that skill.)

For each step, consider the following:

- Who will be the lead?

- What are you going to do?

- By when?

- What will be different to help you recognize that you are successful?

Record your action plan on the action planning worksheet. Two are included here in case you're working on more than one skill.

Action Planning Worksheet

Skill:

ACTION STEP	BY WHOM?	BY WHEN?	MEASURE OF SUCCESS?

Action Planning Worksheet

Skill:

ACTION STEP	BY WHOM?	BY WHEN?	MEASURE OF SUCCESS?

10

Reflections and Closing

What is your most important takeaway that you would like to work on from today's discussion?

How will you use this learning back at work?

Our world becomes a better place to live in every time a team improves its functioning. Your improved skills spill over and influence countless others. Thanks for your good work and good luck!

Resources

Organization

Collaborative Growth®

Visit our websites at www.TheEmotionallyIntelligentTeam.com and www.cgrowth.com to join our ezine list, find tips for building team skills, and to learn more about the TESI®.

Further Reading

Bar-On, R. (2005). *The Bar-On model of emotional-social intelligence (ESI).* Available at www.eiconsortium.org

Hughes, M. (2006). *Life's 2% solution.* London: Nicholas Brealey.

Hughes, M., Patterson, B., & Terrell, J.B. (2005). *Emotional intelligence in action: Training and coaching activities for leaders and managers.* San Francisco, CA: Pfeiffer.

Hughes, M., & Terrell, J.B. (2007). *The emotionally intelligent team.* San Francisco, CA: Jossey-Bass.

Hughes, M., & Terrell, J.B. (2008). *A coach's guide to emotional intelligence.* San Francisco, CA: Pfeiffer.

Marcia Hughes is president of Collaborative Growth®, LLC. and serves as a strategic communications partner for teams and their leaders in organizations that value high performers. She weaves her expertise in emotional intelligence throughout her consulting work, facilitation, team building, and workshops to help people motivate themselves and communicate more effectively with others. Her keynotes are built around powerful stories of how success can grow when people work collaboratively. Businesses, government agencies, and nonprofits have all benefited in such areas as team and leadership development, strategic design, and conflict resolution from her proven formula for success. She is co-author of *A Coach's Guide to Emotional Intelligence* (2008), *The Emotionally Intelligent Team* (2007), *Emotional Intelligence in Action* (2005), and author of *Life's 2% Solution* (2006).

Ms. Hughes is a certified trainer in the Bar-On EQ-i and EQ-360. She provides train-the-trainer training and coaching in powerful EQ delivery. Her efforts to improve productivity in the workplace through strategic communication grew out of a distinguished career in law, in which her firm specialized in complex public policy matters. There again, her leadership and communication skills enabled Hughes's team to effectively address controversial environmental, land use, and water development matters involving numerous stakeholders, which included federal, state, and local governments, along with the general public.

As an assistant attorney general, she served the Department of Public Health and the Environment. She clerked on the 10th Circuit Court of Appeals for the Honorable William E. Doyle.

James Bradford Terrell is vice president of Collaborative Growth®. LLC, where he applies his expertise in interpersonal communication to help a variety of public- and private-sector clients anticipate change and respond to it resiliently.

Co-author of *A Coach's Guide to Emotional Intelligence* (2008), *The Emotionally Intelligent Team* (2007), and *Emotional Intelligence in Action* (2005), he coaches leaders, teams in transition, and senior management, using the Bar-On EQ-i®, the EQ-360®, and other assessments. Mr. Terrell provides train-the-trainer workshops and educates coaches on how to develop the insightful interpretation and application of EQ results. He also works as a consultant and contract mediator for the U.S. Forest Service and other federal agencies.

He worked as a psychotherapist in private practice for many years and served as executive director of the Syntropy Institute, a not-for-profit research organization investigating how communication training impacts human effectiveness. He also served as the director of training for the Metro-Denver Mutual Housing Association, an early developer of cooperative housing in the Denver area.

In a previous life, he was the owner/operator of Integrity Building Systems, a construction company specializing in residential and commercial renovation, and served as a project coordinator on a wide variety of building projects, including Denver International Airport and the National Digital Cable Television Center. In a future life he is certain he will be a rock star.